THE DEAD SEA SCROLLS

JOEL WILLITTS

Contents

Kregel
Publications

Caves, Scrolls and Christians

What are the Dead Sea Scrolls?

The phrase 'Dead Sea Scrolls' might conjure up archaeological treasure in the hands of Indiana Jones or something out of *Tomb Raider* – or perhaps an image of clay pots, musty manuscripts and dusty old caves.

The scrolls were found, as their name suggests, in the Dead Sea region of Israel. The Dead Sea is a body of water about 20 km (13 miles) east of Jerusalem and 15 km (9 miles) south of Jericho, connected to the Sea of Galilee in northern Israel by the Jordan River. The Dead Sea has no outlet, so because the region is one of the driest and hottest places on earth – in addition to being the lowest (about 800 metres or 1300 feet below sea level) – its water evaporates rapidly, making it the saltiest natural body of water in the world, 10 times saltier than the ocean, with a 30 per cent salt content. The extraordinary atmosphere in the Dead Sea Valley provided the perfect climate for ancient scrolls to survive over a very long period of time. If the scrolls had been stored elsewhere, it is doubtful they would have survived for 2000 years.

As their name implies, the 'Dead Sea Scrolls' are ancient documents of parchment and papyrus. They are different from a book (or *codex*) because a scroll rolls out and is not written on bound pages that can be turned. Leather and papyrus scrolls were the medium of written works in the first century BC and AD; what we know today as 'books' did not come into use until the late first and early second century AD.

In caves along the Dead Sea Valley, on the fringe of the Judean Desert, around ancient ruins called Khirbet Qumran (*Khirbet* is Arabic for 'ruin'), a dozen scrolls were discovered, along with innumerable fragments of papyrus and parchment. Together these scrolls and fragments represent more than 800 original documents, written mostly in Hebrew, a smaller number in Aramaic, and a few in ancient Greek.

A unique exception to the papyrus and parchment was the discovery of the Copper Scroll, made of copper with the text engraved on it. The Copper Scroll is a treasure map of locations which supposedly contain gold, silver, coins, vessels, priestly garments and more scrolls. Naturally, scholars looked for these treasures – but never found any. If the treasure did exist at one time, it has long since been removed.

Aerial view of the Jordan River flowing through the rift valley into the Dead Sea.

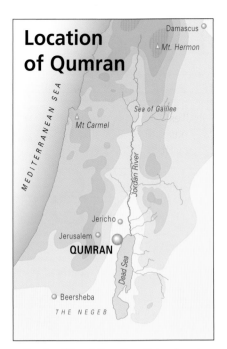

Location of Qumran

So the 'Dead Sea Scrolls' refers to a large ancient library of scrolls found in 11 caves along the shore of the Dead Sea, near Khirbet Qumran. Each cave is identified by a number – Cave 1, Cave 2, etc. Archaeologists also found scrolls at other sites in the Dead Sea Valley, or Judean Desert, in six locations at Masada, Nahal Hever (Wadi Khabra), Nahal Seelim (Wadi Seigal), Wadi Murabba´at, Nahai Mishmar (Wadi Mahras), and Nahal Hemar. Together, the scrolls found in these seven locations are known as the 'Judean Desert Scrolls', though in this survey we will not discuss non-Qumran scrolls.

Why should Christians study the scrolls?

1. The scrolls confirm the trustworthiness of the canon of the Old Testament.
The scrolls contain either the whole, or portions, of every book in the Protestant Old Testament except the book of Esther. So the Hebrew text (called by scholars the Masoretic Text or 'MT' for short) that was used to make the Old Testament we read today reflects the Hebrew Scriptures found in the scrolls at Qumran. Prior to finding the Qumran scrolls, the earliest Hebrew text we possessed of the Old

Testament came from the Middle Ages (about AD 1000). The scrolls found near the Dead Sea, then, support the Old Testament text we read today and, at the very least, assure us that the text of our Old Testament is trustworthy and has not been altered by later scribes.

2. The content of the Dead Sea Scrolls helps fill a significant gap in our knowledge of Judaism at the time of Jesus.

Some 400 years of Jewish history fall between the end of the Old Testament (Malachi) and the beginning of the New Testament, and the historical and theological developments of those 'silent years' had a significant effect on the formation of the New Testament. The Gospel writers, Paul, and the others wrote within the parameters of first-century Judaism. Jesus' work of redemption and the New Testament writers' narration and interpretation of those events took place within a particular ancient Jewish thought-world. So, the better we understand the historical and theological context in which Jesus and the New Testament writers lived, the better we will understand the meaning and significance of the Gospel.

This is where the study of the Dead Sea Scrolls comes in. The scrolls are documents that first-century Jewish people composed and read before and during the time of Jesus. They provide unparalleled background material for filling in the gaps left by the Gospel writers, gaps that relate to first-century Jewish customs and controversies that we see reflected in the Gospels. The scrolls give us an 'insider's look' at Palestinian Judaism.

There are, it is true, other Jewish sources that provide information on first-century Jewish life, history, and thought, such as the Old Testament Pseudepigrapha (see p. 10), the Aramaic Targumim, and the Mishnah. These documents, though,

Artist's depiction of the Copper Scroll found near Khirbet Qumran.

while containing material derived from the first century, were composed centuries later. In contrast, the Dead Sea Scrolls were all composed between 300 BC and AD 70 and are our most reliable historical and theological source for the New Testament period.

3. The Dead Sea Scrolls teach us that our Christian faith is rooted in Judaism.

The scrolls found in the caves around Qumran remind us what the New Testament takes for granted, but what we often do not realize: Christianity and Judaism were and are organically linked, in the past, present and future (see Romans 9–11). The scrolls teach us that Christianity did not begin as a separate religion, as we regard it today.

The early Christians were Jewish and their writings – which eventually came together into the canon of the New Testament – would have been considered as the 'Jewish writings' of a Messianic movement. Jewish people in the first century called a movement such as early Christianity a sect (see Acts 24:5, 'the sect of the Nazarenes'). The term 'sect' is just another way of referring to a 'faction' or 'party', and there were several different sects among Palestinian Jews (see below, pp. 20, 22-23). Jesus was himself a law-observing Jew, as were his first followers and believers. In fact, they did not even call themselves 'Christians', but were given that name by outsiders in Antioch (Acts 11:26). The early Christians did not think themselves to be anything other than Jewish believers in Jesus.

How do the Dead Sea Scrolls teach us about the Jewishness of our Christian faith? They attest that the group who stored them in the caves were, like the early Christians, a Jewish Messianic sect – which makes it possible, by comparing the two groups, better to understand the Jewish aspects of early Christianity. For example, there may be beliefs and practices that we thought uniquely Christian that are actually common to both the Dead Sea Scrolls community and to early Christianity. It is tempting to focus on how *different* the Qumran Community is from Christianity – and on many points, there are indeed great differences. Yet, beyond the oddity of the group, their underlying beliefs about God, Messiah, the nature of God's people and the future, and even some of their practices, overlap significantly with the New Testament.

The more we learn about the views and practices of the community of the Dead Sea Scrolls, the better we may understand not merely the Jewish context within which Christianity was born, but the very teachings of Jesus and beliefs of the New Testament writers. Our own faith can deepen as we appreciate and embrace the Jewishness of the Christian faith.

The Discovery of the Scrolls

In the winter of 1946–47 a teenage Bedouin goat-herd named Muhammad ed-Dib ('the Wolf') went hunting with a couple of his friends for a stray goat in the cliffs near the northwest shore of the Dead Sea. On the edge of the Judean Desert, Muhammad found a cave he thought his goat had entered. He threw a stone into the cave and heard the sound of a clay pot breaking. Intrigued, he and his friends entered the cave and stumbled across ten uniquely-shaped clay jars. Opening a couple of the jars, they found seven scrolls wrapped in linen cloth. Although they couldn't recognize the ancient script on the scrolls, they thought their find might be worth something, so they packed the scrolls and clay pots away, planning to sell them to an antiquities dealer when the opportunity arose.

Depiction of one of the uniquely shaped clay pots in which some of the Dead Sea Scrolls were discovered.

Valuable scrolls

In March 1947 Muhammad showed his finds to a cobbler-cum-antiquities dealer named Kando in Bethlehem. Kando was puzzled by the script on the scrolls and sought the assistance of the head of St. Mark's Monastery in Bethlehem, Mar Athanasius Yeshua Samuel. The scrolls impressed Mar Samuel who, though no expert on ancient Semitic languages, believed them to be valuable and purchased four of them from Kando in July. Mean-while, two of the remaining scrolls were shown to a professor at the Hebrew University, named Eleazar L. Sukenik, who immediately recognized the age and value of the scrolls and concluded that they were a very significant find. By the end of 1947, he had bought the remaining three scrolls for the university. On 26 April 1948, Sukenik announced publicly that he possessed the scrolls, and in 1955, less than eight years after acquiring them, he published his scrolls.

This early discovery, acquisition and publishing of the scrolls took place during a turbulent time in the history of Palestine. Since 1922 the region had been under a British Mandate. However, on 29 November 1947, the United Nations voted in favour of the partition of Palestine between Jews and Arabs. This decision resulted in the establishment of the independent State of Israel on 14 May 1948, and later to what has become known as the 'Six-Day War', in 1967. During these decades the political situation was unstable and movement in and around Jerusalem was often very dangerous. In spite of this, scholars such as Sukenik took great personal risks to acquire and publish the scrolls.

Israeli archaeologist Professor Eleazar Sukenik who was shown two of the scrolls as early as 1947.

Selling the scrolls

Meanwhile in February 1948, Mar Samuel showed three of his scrolls to members of the American School of Oriental Research (ASOR) based in Jerusalem. The resident scholars – John Trever, William Brownlee and the school's director Millar Burrows – photographed and studied them, and on 12 April 1948 ASOR released a statement to the *Times* of London announcing the monumental discovery. Three years later, ASOR published three of Mar Samuel's scrolls. Mar Samuel took his scrolls to the USA, where on 1 June 1954 he placed an advertisement in the *Wall Street Journal* offering for sale 'The Four Dead Sea Scrolls'. They were eventually purchased by Yigael Yadin, on behalf of the State of Israel, for $250,000.

So by 1956, less than a decade after their discovery, the seven scrolls found in Cave 1 had been acquired by the State of Israel and published. An archaeological initiative was also undertaken in the early years of the scroll discoveries. After Cave 1 was

In caves in these weathered sandstone cliffs near the shore of the Dead Sea at Khirbet Qumran many of the Dead Sea Scrolls were discovered.

re-discovered in January 1949 by Captain Philippe Lippens, a Belgian soldier with the United Nations Armistice Observer Corps, an excavation of the cave was undertaken between 15 February and 5 March 1949 by G. Lankester Harding, Director of the Jordanian Antiquities Authority, and Father Roland de Vaux, Director of the French École Biblique in Jerusalem. De Vaux became most famous for his excavation of the settlement at Khirbet Qumran, which uncovered pottery, pieces of linen cloth, and other artifacts, as well as fragments from additional manuscripts. Some of these fragments were from the same manuscripts that the Bedouin goat-herds had removed from the cave, thus confirming that the

original scrolls were indeed taken from there.

The search continues
The discovery of the scrolls in Cave 1 by the Bedouin initiated an all-out search for more caves and scrolls. The Bedouin consistently outwitted the scholars as they continued to find new caves and unearth artifacts; for them it was a lucrative business, as they subsequently sold their finds for good money. Scholars had to play catch-up, trying to ensure that the caves and scrolls were preserved for research. By 1956, 11 significant caves had been discovered around Khirbet Qumran. The most important was Cave 4, just metres from the settlement. This man-made cave

was hewn out of the marl terrace apparently for the express purpose of housing scrolls. Scholars found the remains of 550 documents in this cave, broken up into thousands of fragments. For many reasons – some discussed on p. 7 – only as recently as 2004, some five decades after their discovery, were the last documents finally published. Today all the scrolls from the 11 caves have been edited and published and are available for study.

The Scholars and the Scrolls

Since the moment ancient scrolls began appearing on the antiquities market in Jerusalem in the middle of the last century, scholars have been keenly interested in – even obsessed with – the Dead Sea Scrolls.

Scrolls rediscovered

Although the scrolls were re-discovered in the second half of the twentieth century, scholars had known for centuries of the existence of ancient biblical and non-biblical scrolls near Jericho. As early as the third century AD, the Christian theologian and scholar Origen (AD 185–284), commented that, in making his edition of the Old Testament, he had used a text from a jar from a cave near Jericho. Also, the pioneer church historian Eusebius of Caesarea (AD 260–340) records the story of the discovery of a Psalms scroll and other Hebrew and Greek manuscripts in a jar near Jericho during the reign of the Roman Emperor Caracalla (AD 211–17).

500 years later, in the ninth century, a learned bishop called Timothy I from Seleucia (in modern Iraq) wrote about the discovery of 'some books' in a rock dwelling near Jericho. He relates that an Arab hunter, having found the books, went to Jerusalem and informed the Jews of their existence, after which many Jews came and 'found the books of the Old Testament and other writings, in the Hebrew language'.

More recently, in 1896 a British scholar named Solomon Schechter retrieved a collection of medieval manuscripts from a synagogue in the old city of Cairo, Egypt. Among these manuscripts were two fragments of a Jewish document outlining the organization and ideology of a Jewish sect. He named these 'Fragments of a Zadokite Work', because they mention the priestly family of Zadok (see 1 Kings 2:35; 1 Chronicles 29:22; Ezra 7:2; Ezekiel 48:11). Later scholars changed its name to the 'Damascus Document', since the place-name Damascus also appears in the work. Remarkably, 10 different copies of this work were later found in Caves 4, 5, and 6 at Qumran. Scholars now think it is likely that the founder of the medieval Jewish sect known as the Qaraites, to whom the Cairo synagogue belonged, discovered the scroll in the Judean Desert and established an anti-rabbinic sect that flourished from the tenth to thirteenth centuries AD.

So the accidental discovery of Cave 1 by a teenage Bedouin goat-herd, which has been called 'the greatest manuscript find of all time', perhaps also marks the greatest archaeological and scholarly failure of all time. For centuries, scholars possessed evidence that suggested the presence of ancient biblical scrolls in caves in the Judean Desert – but no one set out to find them. This scholarly failure was then overshadowed by the unbelievable mishaps of the first half-century of scroll studies.

Controversy and the scrolls

While the scrolls found in Cave 1 were all published within a decade of their discovery and the scrolls from Caves 2, 3, and 5–10 were published by 1962, Cave 4 proved to be different.

International team

The large amount of material found in Cave 4, coupled with the very poor condition of the fragments, led Roland de Vaux to set up an international editorial committee of eight men in the spring of 1953, including Jozef T. Milik (Polish, Roman Catholic), Frank M. Cross (American, Presbyterian), John

A fragment from one of the Dead Sea Scrolls.

Aerial view of the Judean Desert. The Dead Sea can be seen top right.

Marco Allegro (British, agnostic), John Strugnell (British, Presbyterian, but later converted to Catholicism), Claus-Hunno Hunzinger (German, Lutheran; later replaced by Maurice Baillet – French, Roman Catholic), J. Starcky (French, Roman Catholic), and Patrick Skehan (American, Roman Catholic). The most glaring absence from this list was an Israeli representative – an absence all the more remarkable considering that most of the scrolls were written in Hebrew, the mother tongue of Israelis – and that they address not Christian but Jewish history. Not until decades later were Israelis invited to join the team.

Because of the size of the project, financial backing was sought to underwrite the editors' work. The most significant donation was from the American philanthropist John D. Rockefeller, who in 1954 provided enough money to fund the committee's work for six years. In addition, educational and religious institutions were solicited to buy the scrolls: after the experts had edited and published them, these institutions would have taken possession of the scrolls. However, these institutions never took delivery, because in 1960 the Jordanian government reimbursed them for the scrolls and housed them instead in the Palestine Archaeological Museum, now called the Rockefeller Museum, in Jerusalem.

Incompetence

The early decisions of de Vaux and others caused havoc in later years, leading to suspicions of academic scandal. In fact, there were no conspiracies or scandals, only incompetence and scholarly pride on the part of the initial editorial team. Once the original editors received their allotment of Cave 4 scrolls, it became each editor's intellectual property and was selfishly hoarded. The task was enormous, and de Vaux should not have divided it between so few individuals.

Eventually the funding for the project dried up and the scholars had to return to their sending academic institutions, where university life invaded and further slowed the editing and publishing process. Moreover, some of the original team had to give up their roles for health reasons. When de Vaux, the editor-in-chief of the *Discoveries of the Judean Desert (DJD)*, the official scholarly publication of the scrolls, died in 1971, a specialist named Pierre Benoit replaced him.

The result of the mismanagement of the editorial process was that only one publication from Cave 4 appeared between its discovery in 1952 and the early 1990s, nearly five decades later. This delay was unacceptable both to the scholarly community and to the general public. In the late 1980s, pressure began to mount against the editorial team. In 1984, Pierre Benoit resigned and, following the brief and unproductive editorship of John Strugnell, Emmanuel Tov of the Hebrew University in Jerusalem was appointed editor-in-chief of *DJD*. Tov's first move was to expand the editorial team to approximately 60 members, which now included Jewish scholars, although Tov maintained the policy of allowing his team exclusive access to the scrolls, a policy he inherited from his predecessors and the Israel Antiquities Authority (IAA), who now provided oversight of the work.

Publication completed

But a series of events between 1990 and 1992 culminated in the release of photographic negatives of all the Cave 4 scrolls by the Huntington Library in San Marino, California. After this, all the manuscripts from Cave 4 were accessible to any qualified scholar interested in the scrolls and able to read ancient Hebrew, Aramaic, and Greek. No longer were they under the exclusive control of a few. In the decade that followed, scholars published several different English translations and textual editions. Finally, more than a decade later, the official scholarly publication of the scrolls, *DJD*, was complete.

Discoveries of the Judean Desert (DJD), along with other scroll editions, both electronic and printed, make possible the study of the scrolls in their entirety. The first stage of research ended with the publication of *DJD*, and the comprehensive study of the meaning of the Dead Sea Scrolls began.

Dating the Scrolls

Period	Number of Manuscripts
Archaic (250–150 BC)	21 mss
Archaic to Hasmonean (200–150 BC)	20 mss
Hasmonean (150–30 BC)	224 mss
Transition to Herodian (ca. 75–1 BC)	5 mss
Herodian (50 or 30 BC–AD 68)	418 mss

Only 11 of the more than 800 documents making up the Dead Sea Scrolls were found in a well-preserved state. Although a few scrolls were found in clay jars, most were found either in carved niches inside cave walls or on the ground beneath layers of dust. Due to the elements, rats, insects, fungus, and human activity, most of the scrolls were badly damaged. Cave 1 stands out for its well-preserved scrolls. So the English translation of the scrolls that you might pick up and read represents documents formed from countless fragments.

Dating the scrolls

The dating of the scrolls found at Qumran was of fundamental importance. Accurate dating is essential, since the proper interpretation of the scrolls hinges on their historical context. The period of the composition of the scrolls is almost universally agreed by scholars today as between the third century (300–200) BC and first century AD. Arguments from four areas have established this:
1. *Archaeology.*
2. *Palaeography.*
3. *Carbon-14 dating.*
4. *Historical allusions in the scrolls.*

Since 1 and 4 are discussed below, we will not go into them here, except to state that both support the time-span given above.

Palaeography
James VanderKam and Peter Flint define palaeography as 'the science that investigates the styles of ancient handwriting, that is, the ways in which scribes formed letters, and the evolutionary changes in those styles over time as a means for establishing a relative

chronology of texts'.[1] Palaeography is as much an art as a science and can only provide an approximate range of dating. Many of the writings of antiquity, and no less from Qumran, were created by professional scribes, who would have been trained in a standard way of forming letters. These scribes would have followed the contemporary style of writing. Given what we know of scribal practice, changes in scripts would have taken time to occur.

The foremost expert on Dead Sea Scrolls palaeography is Frank M. Cross, an original member of the editorial team. Cross's work on the scrolls led him to distinguish three periods for the scripts found in the scrolls:
1. **Archaic Period**, ca. 250–150 BC – mostly biblical texts
2. **Hasmonean Period**, ca. 150–30 BC – he considered this the 'heyday of sectarian composition'
3. **Herodian Period**, ca. 30 BC – AD 70

Cross's results have been tabulated to show that almost all the scrolls from the caves at Qumran were copied in the Hasmonean and Herodian periods (see box above).[2]

Carbon-14 dating
Carbon-14 dating is a complex scientific tool used to date the scrolls. In the early stages of the discoveries, it was not wise to subject the scrolls to a Carbon-14 procedure because it required a significant amount of original scroll material, which it destroyed in the dating process. However, in the 1990s a new method called Accelerator Mass Spectrometry (AMS) testing was developed which

One of the scrolls is painstakingly unravelled in the early days of research.

Professor A. Bieberkraut, of the Hebrew University, Jerusalem, and Dr Avigad work to restore one of the Dead Sea Scrolls.

used much less material. So, in 1991 and again in 1994–95, sets of scrolls were subjected to AMS analysis. The results of all the tests – both in the early days of the discoveries and in the last decade of the twentieth century – provide independent confirmation of Cross's conclusion that the scrolls were composed in the last two centuries BC and the first century AD.

Reconstructing the scrolls

Specialists set about reconstructing the scrolls from the thousands of manuscript fragments collected from the caves, especially from Cave 4 – a process crucial to establishing the text.

In the scrollery
The first editors of the Dead Sea Scrolls worked in a room known as the 'scrollery' in the Rockefeller Museum in Jerusalem. As mounds of fragments came in, the editors' first task was to sift through them, attempting to piece documents together. They would first group fragments based on general appearance and the colour of the leather, the thickness and preparation of the skin, the dimensions of the manuscript, the columns, margins, and rulings, the ink, the handwriting, the degree of care of the scribe, and the spelling.

Next the fragments were organized into a text that makes sense. This process took great patience. It was easier if the text being worked on was already known, such as a biblical scroll. However, often the editors were looking at fragments of unknown texts that required reconstruction without any guide – rather like putting together a complex 5000-piece jigsaw puzzle without a box-top picture.

Unrecognizable texts
A German scholar named Hartmut Stegemann developed a method – appropriately called the 'Stegemann Method' – to help with unrecognizable texts. His method focused on the form and appearance of the manuscript rather than on the writing, paying close attention to the damage pattern of the fragments of the scroll. Hebrew scrolls unroll from right to left, with the beginning of the text on the outside right. On a damaged scroll, the distance between the damage pattern decreases progressively from the beginning of the text (the outer, right side of the scroll) toward the end (the inner, left side). With this information, one can trace the damage patterns and thus reconstruct the text of the scroll.

Debatable decisions
It should be clear that the final form of some of the scrolls, especially those previously unknown, is hypothetical. The editor who reconstructed a particular scroll has made many debatable scholarly decisions about the placement of fragments above, beside or below other fragments; if it is papyrus, an attempt has been made to match the direction of the strands of the reed. In addition, the editor has made a decision about the width of the columns on the scroll, the number of lines in a column, and the number of letters on a line.

All of these are decisions of judgment. We have every reason to trust the competence of the editors of the official publication of the Dead Sea Scrolls (*DJD*), but these reconstructions, although the product of learned experts in the field, are in some places no more than educated guesses. This is just one of many reasons to hold our interpretations of particular scrolls with some humility.

The Qumran Library

The scrolls found in the 11 caves around Khirbet Qumran make up an ancient library with an organized collection of texts.

The library

The Qumran Community did not normally use most of the caves as libraries, but in haste placed the scrolls in them for safekeeping just before the Romans destroyed their settlement in AD 68. Cave 1, the first to be discovered, is quite inaccessibly located high up in the rocky cliffs.

Yet the occupants of Qumran regularly used a few caves for storing their collection of scrolls. Cave 4 is the best example, as it seems to have been specially designed by the community for holding scrolls. Not only was the greatest number of manuscripts found in Cave 4 (the remains of 550 separate scrolls), but also the cave is just a short walk from the settlement site. Inside the main chamber of the cave the walls have holes that were at one time used to help support wooden shelves for the scrolls. The shelves have long since rotted and collapsed, leaving the scrolls to fall to the cave floor, exposing them to the ravages of the elements for nearly two millennia – probably a major reason for the poor condition of the scrolls found in this cave.

A filing system?

One scholar has suggested that the Qumran Community had an organized library filing system, since the collection of scrolls can be divided into three categories:
1. *Old Testament* (biblical) documents
2. *Apocrypha and Pseudepigrapha*
3. *Unique sectarian documents* composed by the community (see pp. 13–15).

1. Old Testament

About a quarter of the scrolls found (c. 200 manuscripts) were biblical texts, representing every book of the Old Testament except Esther.

Textual fluidity

The biblical manuscripts from the Dead Sea Scrolls reveal the interesting and surprising fact that in the first century different editions of the Hebrew and Greek Scriptures were in circulation – in other words, 'textual fluidity' existed. This is very different from today: while we possess a number of different English translations and versions of the Hebrew text – for example *New Living Translation, New International Version, New Revised Standard Version, New American Standard Bible* etc. – they are all based on the *same* Hebrew text, the Masoretic Text or MT.

Inspiration

We should never think that any of today's versions is the 'inspired' Word of God itself. They are simply translations and, as such, interpretations of the same Hebrew text. Even the *one* Hebrew text upon which we base our translations is not inspired. Rather, we believe that the original autographs, which the authors wrote in antiquity, are the

---

Canon
The word 'canon' literally means 'reed' or 'measuring tool'. When we speak of the Old Testament or New Testament canon, we mean the list of writings that the church has recognised as inspired Scripture. The Protestant canon consists of 39 books in the Old Testament and 26 in the New Testament. Other Christian traditions differ on the extent of the canon, with the Catholic and Orthodox churches including more books in the Old Testament canon.

Apocrypha
'Apocrypha' refers to books or parts of books that do not appear in the Hebrew Bible (or Protestant), but do appear in the Jewish Scriptures in Greek, called the Septuagint (and in Roman Catholic and Christian Orthodox Bibles).

An early 'codex' or book – see p. 2.

Pseudepigrapha 'Pseudepigrapha' refers to ancient Jewish works outside the Old Testament, the Apocrypha, and the works of Philo and Josephus that were mostly known to us before the discovery of the scrolls.

One common factor for both the Apocrypha and Pseudepigrapha is that neither are included in the Bible by many Christians – Catholic Bibles do include some of these works, which they call the deutero-canonical writings. However, in the Second Temple period (the time after the writing of Malachi in the fourth century BC and before the New Testament) there was not a clearly defined 'canon' of Scripture as there is today. Many of the books that are in our Old Testament had a 'canon-like' status and were held as sacred Scripture by all Jews. But some of the books we think of as outside the canon, some Jews and even early Christians thought of as no less inspired than, say, Genesis or Isaiah.

Also during this period the Bible seems to have been divided into three divisions: the Law (Genesis–Deuteronomy), Prophets (the major and minor prophets and some of the historical books) and other writings (poetry, usually attributed to David).

In order to follow the command of this passage, Jews of the first century wrote down the words of the Law on pieces of parchment and placed them in small containers. When these containers were put on doorposts they were called *mezuzot*. When they were placed on the arm or forehead they were referred to as phylacteries (*tefillin* in Hebrew, which means 'prayer'). Both *mezuzot* and phylacteries were found at Qumran.

These two Jews have phylacteries on their foreheads and arms.

2. Apocrypha and Pseudepigrapha

About half the manuscripts found among the scrolls (c. 400 manuscripts) are texts now regarded as either Apocrypha or Pseudepigrapha (see box opposite). These terms designate Jewish texts composed during the Second Temple period that were significant for Jews, but for us are not canonical. We knew of many of these texts before the discovery of the scrolls, but a few were discovered for the first time at Qumran. They are not sectarian, but embody ideas held by a large circle of Jews and probably circulated broadly within Palestinian Judaism.

The following previously known texts were found among the scrolls:

This *mezuza* contains a small parchment with a Bible text.

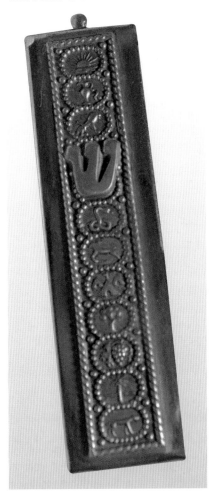

only inspired texts. While these original texts have not survived the thousands of years of intervening history, they have been carefully copied through the ages by scribes, like those among the community of Qumran. Therefore, the MT, while not the inspired text, is a very trustworthy representation of God's original inspired Scripture.

However, in ancient times Jews considered these different editions as equally representative of inspired Scripture, and it doesn't seem that the differences concerned them. The evidence of textual fluidity presents us with interesting possibilities and questions about the Bible in ancient times, questions which become especially important when studying the New Testament's use of the Old Testament. For instance, one can justifiably ask: 'Which Hebrew or Greek edition is the New Testament writer quoting?'

Old Testament references come in the form of full biblical scrolls, but also as biblical commentaries called *Pesharim*, quotations in non-biblical texts, Aramaic translations called Targumim, phylacteries (*tefillin*), and *mezuzot* (see box on the *Shema* above).

Text columns from one of the Dead Sea Scrolls exhibited at the Shrine of the Book in Jerusalem.

Tobit

An exciting story about a Jewish exile named Tobit who displays faithfulness to God amid difficult circumstances. The unknown Jewish author of the fable probably wrote it in the fourth or third century BC.

The Wisdom of Ben Sira (also called Sirach or Ecclesiasticus)

Jesus ben Sira was a Jewish teacher who collected wise sayings and instructions between 190 and 180 BC. Before the Judean scrolls were found, this work only survived in Greek.

Enoch

Scholars consider this a Jewish apocalypse. (An apocalypse is a revelation of the mysteries of God, such as Daniel and Revelation.) As is common to this type of writing, the unknown author used the name of a biblical character, Enoch (Genesis 5:21–24). This work was most likely composed in the second-century BC. It is interesting that the Qumran Community treated this book as Scripture.

Jubilees

This is another Jewish apocalypse, retelling much of the biblical history contained in Genesis and Exodus. This type of literature is often referred to as the 'rewritten Bible', because, as the term suggests, the content is a reworking of the biblical material. The revelation purports to have been given by an angel to Moses while he was on Mount Sinai for forty days (Exodus 24:18); however, it was probably composed around 160 BC.

Testaments of the Twelve Patriarchs

This work is known in its 'Christianized' form in the Septuagint. Although no complete copy or individual testament was found at Qumran, parts of it were discovered among the fragments. The whole work presents the imagined last words of Jacob's twelve sons, the ancestors of the twelve tribes of Israel. The writers of these testaments wished to encourage and teach their fellow Jews.

Additional Psalms (Psalms 151, 154, and 155)

Additional Psalms of David were found among the scrolls.

In addition to these previously known texts, excavators found several unknown texts among the scrolls that fall into the category of Apocrypha and Pseudepigrapha as 'rewritten Bible' literature. Among them is the *Genesis Apocryphon*, which contains expanded stories from the book of Genesis. In addition, numerous works focus on biblical characters – including the *Prayer of Nabonidus* and the *Psalms of Joshua*.

Sectarian Texts
in the Library

Some Sectarian Texts

Perhaps the most fascinating category of scrolls from Qumran is the texts that were completely unknown before the Dead Sea discovery – writings that display a new and distinctive perspective. Among these manuscripts are foundational documents of a unique sectarian group, a description of a new Temple, collections of songs and hymns, a military manual for the final battle between the 'Sons of Light' and the 'Sons of Darkness', and interpretations of Old Testament prophetic books. These documents, comprising about a quarter of the total found in the caves (c. 200 manuscripts), give a glimpse of the theological beliefs, history and organizational structure of a Jewish group that existed during the last century BC and the first century AD, and make a unique contribution to the study of Judaism in the New Testament era.

Professor Yigael Yadin deciphering a fragment from the Dead Sea Scrolls.

Manuscript Identification

Identifying a manuscript among the scrolls can be very confusing. Up till now we have identified the scrolls only by their colloquial name, for example, the *Genesis Apocryphon*. Some scrolls are also known by a code name: the *Genesis Apocryphon* is also known as 1QApGen. This designation can be broken down as follows: 1Q = Cave 1; ApGen = code name: *Genesis Apocryphon*. The 'Q' is the cave where the manuscript was found and the 'ApGen' is the code name for the manuscript.

Another example of a code name is the Isaiah Scroll from Cave 1, known as 1QIsa^a: '1Q' = Cave 1; 'Isa' = the book of Isaiah; the '^{a}' = the first of two or more manuscripts of the same document.

In addition to the colloquial name and a code name, most of the documents have a number; for example, the biblical commentary on Hosea: the code is 4QpHos^{a-b}: '4Q' = Cave 4; 'pHos' = pesher (commentary) on Hosea; '$^{a-b}$' = two manuscripts. The number is 4Q166–167.

For a complete list of the scrolls found in the caves consult one of the introductions to the scrolls listed on p. 36.

The most important of the sectarian scrolls are:

The Damascus Document
(CD 'Cairo Damascus', 4Q266–72)

The Damascus Document, mentioned previously, was first discovered not at Qumran (see p. 6) but in a synagogue in Cairo, Egypt, in the late 1800s. In the late 1950s, excavators found 10 fragmentary copies of the same document in caves around Qumran. No one knows definitely how a copy of the document reached Egypt; the most likely explanation is that the medieval Jewish Qaraites sect, to whom the Cairo synagogue belonged, took it there from the Judean Desert. The fact that there were so many copies at Qumran suggests it was a very important document for the Qumran Community. Yet this is curious, since the text is addressed to people

Remains of the scriptorium at Qumran.

who live in various towns and villages throughout Israel.

The contents of the document can be divided into two parts: the 'Admonitions' and the 'Laws'. The Admonitions address the group's early history and challenge its members to remain faithful to God by obeying certain rules. A warning at the end exhorts members to obey the strict law code it advocates. In part two, the authors list the laws in question, which address such issues as the priesthood, skin disease, crops, purity and impurity, oaths, marriages, business transactions, the Sabbath, the Temple and Temple city, Gentiles, and foods.

The Rule of the Community
(1QS, 4QS^{a–j}/4Q255–64, 5Q11)[3]

The Cave 1 copy of the *Community Rule* is a nearly complete manuscript, while scholars

> Thus, all the men who entered the new covenant in the land of Damascus and turned and betrayed and departed from the well of living waters, shall not be counted in the assembly of the people, they shall not be inscribed in their lists, from the day of the gathering in of the teacher.
> *CD 19:33–35*

discovered ten additional fragmentary copies in Cave 4 and one in Cave 5. These copies reveal that there was more than one edition of the text circulating within the community, though scholars are unsure why. Possibly the different versions of the *Community Rule* reflect different stages in the history of the community. The Cave 1 edition of the *Community Rule* can be divided into at least five sections:

1. *A description of the community:* its nature, purpose, initiation procedure, annual covenant renewal ceremony, and prayer (1:1–3:12)

2. *A discussion of the Two Spirits:* an explanation of the community's dualistic and predestinarian views, which focus on good and evil in the world (3:13–4:26)

3. *General and specific rules for the conduct of the community* (5:1–7:25)

4. *A description of the foundation of the community* (8:1–10:5)

5. *A hymn of praise* offered by the instructor (*maskil* in Hebrew) (10:5–11:22).

Taken together, these sections provide a picture of life within the community and the requirements for individual members, hence this

> All those who enter in the Rule of the Community shall establish a covenant before God in order to carry out all that he commanded and in order not to stray from following him out of any fear, dread, or testing.
> *1QS 1:16–17*

text has been the most influential in understanding the community that lived at Qumran.

The War Scroll
(1QM, 4Q491–96).

The *War Scroll* is a fascinating description of the final war between the 'Sons of Light' and the 'Sons of Darkness'. Part military manual, part theological and liturgical treatise, it instructs about, and predicts aspects of, the eschatological war in which the sons of light defeat the sons of darkness at the end of a forty-year war. The sons of darkness are a host of gentile nations, especially the Romans (called Kittim), who are led by Belial (Satan). The sons of light are the restored tribes of Israel, who will fight alongside God and his angels against the forces of darkness through a series of battles, culminating in a climactic seventh battle, where finally Yahweh will annihilate the forces of evil under Belial and his minions.

The Halakhic Letter
(4QMMT, 4Q394–99)

The name of this text, *halakhic*, is derived from a Hebrew phrase meaning 'some of the works of the Law'. Scholars consider this document to be a letter written by a group of Jewish priests who had

> The first attack by the sons of light will be launched against the lot of the sons of darkness, against the army of Belial, against the band of Edom and of Moab and of the sons of Ashur, who are being helped by the violators of the covenant. The sons of Levi, the sons of Judah and the sons of Benjamin, the exiled sons of light return from the desert of the nations to camp in the desert of Jerusalem.
> *1QM 1:1–2*

separated themselves from the Jerusalem Temple establishment. The reconstructed document can be divided into three sections:

1. A list of Sabbaths and festivals, considered by most scholars to be a separate document and not part of the original letter.

2. A series of twenty legal (*halakhic*) rulings about which the writer and the recipients disagree (these consist of questions of sacrifice, priestly gifts, purity, forbidden marriages, and persons prohibited from entering the Temple).

3. An address to a respected individual, who appears to be a political leader of the nation (most likely a Hasmonean monarch [see p. 20]).

Some scholars believe this text holds the key to the origin of the community that eventually came to live at Qumran. They note that the tone of this letter is moderate; rather than condemning the opposition, the letter seems interested in persuading them to change. Of particular note is the similarity between the legal rulings in this document and beliefs attributed to the Sadducees in later rabbinic texts.

Several sectarian texts include:
The Hodayot (1QH)
The Temple Scroll (11QT)

Also the biblical commentaries, called Pesharim ('interpretation[s]' in Hebrew) are unique:

Pesher Exegesis
The biblical interpretations and commentaries among the scrolls are unique. They interpret the words of the Bible, especially the prophets, to refer to the present experiences of the Community in the Second Temple period.

Pesher Isaiah (3Q4, 4Q161–65)
Pesher Hosea (4Q166–67)
Pesher Micah (1Q14)
Pesher Nahum (4Q169)
Pesher Habakkuk (1QpHab)
Pesher Zephaniah (1Q15, 4Q170)
Pesher Psalms (1Q16, 4Q171, 4Q173)
4QFlorilegium (4Q174)
4QCantena A (4Q177)
Melchizedek (11Q13)

What light do the scrolls shed?

The documents that have come to light in the library of Qumran provide unprecedented insight into first-century Judaism. One of the most important elements has been the presence of texts of virtually the whole Hebrew Bible. These biblical texts have contributed greatly to a better understanding of the textual transmission of the Bible through its early history. The most important two facts from these discoveries are that the Masoretic Text, on which our Old Testament is based, is reliable and that the text is 'fluid' (see p. 11).

First-century Judaism

In addition to the biblical manuscripts, several texts of the Apocrypha and Pseudepigrapha, which had been known only through later Greek translations, have been found at Qumran in the original Hebrew and Aramaic language. These discoveries have verified their importance to Palestinian Judaism, and have shown that the library of Qumran is more representative of the literature of first-century Judaism than has often been recognized.

Sectarian writings

The most intriguing of the texts from the library at Qumran are those which address sectarian concerns. These include rules, commentaries, and letters, and give us an insight into one extreme Jewish faction that existed in first-century Palestine. Yet, the presence of various copies of the rule documents, which represent developing forms of the text, perhaps show that the group developed from a more moderate sect into a much more closed and exclusive one.

A scroll unrolls right to left (see p. 9).

We have written to you some of the works of the Torah which we think are good for you and for your people, for we saw that you have intellect and knowledge of the Law. Reflect on all these matters and seek from him that he may support your counsel and keep far from you the evil scheming and the counsel of Belial, so that at the end of time, you may rejoice in finding that some of our words are true. And it shall be reckoned to you as justice when you do what is upright and good before him, for your good and that of Israel.
4QMMT C26–32

15

Qumran

First excavation

The caves where the scrolls were discovered are close to the archaeological site called Khirbet Qumran. Before the discovery of the scrolls, archaeologists had long been aware of the ruins of Qumran, which were visible as a pile of stones. In 1951, within a few years of the discovery and initial excavation of Cave 1, Roland de Vaux and G. Lankester Harding undertook the first archaeological excavation, which eventually encompassed six campaigns, with the last archaeological season in 1958.

Early on in the excavations, de Vaux and his team decided that the site and the scrolls should be linked. In addition, he claimed that the sect known as the Essenes (see below, pp. 20, 22) occupied the Qumran site continuously for about two centuries, except for a short period after an earthquake in 31 BC. Once these connections were established, de Vaux used the scrolls from Cave 1 and information about the Essenes from ancient Greek sources to assist in his interpretation of the Qumran site. The link between the scrolls and the Essenes became the dominant view among scroll scholars, and although recently this view has been contested, it remains the most widely held, and has recently been reaffirmed with some revision by archaeologist Jodi Magness.[4]

We need to consider the relationship between the scrolls and the site more closely, since it is important to recognize that the scrolls *can* be interpreted without reference to the site. If there had been no Qumran site, the study of the scrolls would go on unabated. Very little, if anything, from the archaeology of the site has shed light on the meaning of the scrolls. More-over, a definitive connection between the caves and scrolls and the site is made difficult by the fact that no scrolls or remains of scrolls were found at the site that could definitely be connected with the caves.

The scrolls and the settlement

By contrast, when we try to interpret the archaeology of Khirbet Qumran, it is virtually impossible to understand the site as a 'sectarian settlement' – the dominant view – without information gleaned from the scrolls. (Which is not to say that there are no archaeological clues at the site itself that justify a sectarian interpretation.) Those who question the consensus view, not least because of the lack of evidence of scrolls at the site, maintain that the site should be read and interpreted

Steps leading into one of the ritual baths or *mikva'ot* at Qumran.

on its own terms without reference to the scrolls. They contend that, when this is done, a very different picture of life at Qumran appears.

Country villa?

Among the scholars who reject the sectarian interpretation of the site, some have claimed it was a country villa, and point to the archaeological remains of fine ware found at Qumran to support their claim.

Archaeologists at work in one of the Qumran caves where Dead Sea Scrolls were discovered.

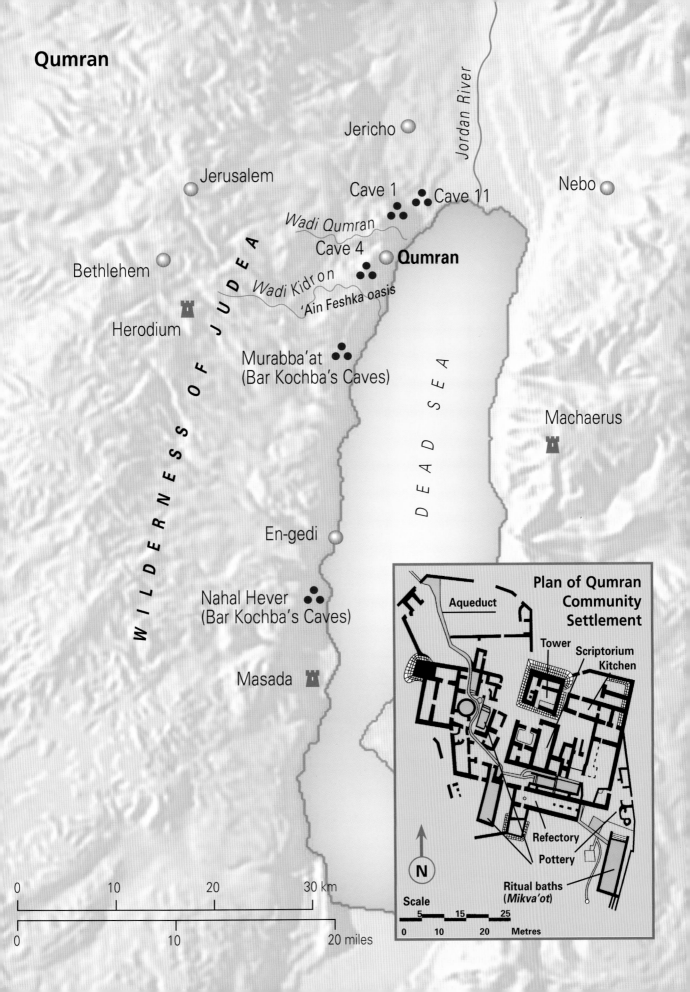

Qumran

Jericho

Jerusalem

Nebo

Cave 1

Cave 11

Wadi Qumran

Cave 4

Qumran

Wadi Kidron

'Ain Feshka oasis

Bethlehem

Herodium

W I L D E R N E S S   O F   J U D E A

Murabba'at
(Bar Kochba's Caves)

Jordan River

D E A D   S E A

Machaerus

En-gedi

Nahal Hever
(Bar Kochba's Caves)

Masada

| 0 | 10 | 20 | 30 km |

| 0 | 10 | 20 miles |

Plan of Qumran Community Settlement

Aqueduct

Tower

Scriptorium

Kitchen

Refectory

Pottery

Ritual baths
(*Mikva'ot*)

N

Scale

| 5 | 15 | 25 |
| 0 | 10 | 20 | Metres |

The reconstructed watchtower at Qumran. Some scholars have suggested that the settlement was originally a fortress.

Others argue from the presence of a tower that the remains suggest a fortress that perhaps the occupants later turned into a fortified villa. However, both these positions need to account for the presence of the scrolls in caves just metres from the site. If the inhabitants of the site did not put the scrolls in the caves, who did?

The most common explanation offered by these dissenting scholars is that the scrolls represent a priestly library that was brought to the caves for safekeeping as the Romans were beginning their siege of Jerusalem in AD 68. This view has certain merits, not least the fact that the collection of scrolls found in the caves is not solely the work of a small sectarian community, but reflects a diversity of viewpoints, while also the scripts on the scrolls reveal a number of scribal hands involved in their production.

All related?

For most scholars, these alternative views do not provide a convincing hypothesis either for the evidence at the site or for the presence of the scrolls nearby. Three pieces of archaeological evidence seem to confirm a relationship between the scrolls, the caves, and the site:

1. The presence of the unusual and now well-known **cylinder scroll jars**. These jars, which are prevalent at Qumran but rare or unattested at other sites, were found both in Cave 1 (nearly 50 jars) and at the settlement site and suggest a link.

2. At Qumran excavators found **inkwells** that suggest scribal activity at the site, with the possibility that the occupants of Qumran composed at least some of the scrolls. Just how many – and which – documents is difficult to determine.

3. The **proximity of the caves,** and especially of Cave 4, to Qumran. As we have seen, Cave 4 was specifically designed for storing scrolls, and appears to have been the main library of the community.

A sectarian settlement?

Evidence found at the site, together with information from the scrolls, suggest that Qumran was a 'sectarian settlement'. Jodi Magness lists three clues that point to its sectarian nature:[5]

1. The **extensive water system** and several **Jewish baths** (Hebrew *mikveh*; plural *mikva'ot*) used for ritual purification.

2. The presence of **dining rooms,** a large number of dining dishes and animal bone deposits seem to point to a community who shared in common meals.

3. The positioning of *mikva'ot* throughout the settlement suggests that the inhabitants of Qumran conceived of their settlement as a series of spaces with various degrees of purity or impurity.

In addition, we should not overlook the evidence for what is called the 'Scriptorium' – a second-floor room apparently containing benches and tables for copying scrolls.

Adjacent to the site is a large cemetery with about 1,200 tombs mostly of males, together with some of women and children. The presence of a cemetery with a large number of graves raises the question of the size of the community that resided at Qumran. Scholars agree that few, if any, of the members of the community actually lived at the settlement, since the rooms and spaces at the site seem to have been devoted to communal life, with very little personal living-space. Based on the number of graves however, it appears that at its height the community numbered nearly 200 members. Probably these members lived nearby either in caves or tents.

Phases of Occupation at Khirbet Qumran

Roland de Vaux believed there were three periods of occupation at the site and scholars continue to follow his scheme, although some have suggested revisions:

Period Ia	The site was constructed in the reign of John Hyrcannus (*ca.* 134–104 BC); Jodi Magness suggests that the site was not occupied at this time
Period Ib	The site was abandoned due to an earthquake *ca.* 100–31 BC; Magness suggests a pre-earthquake phase (100–50 BC, to 31 BC) and post-earthquake phase (from 31 BC to 9/8 BC or some time thereafter)
Period II	Restoration under Herod Archelaus (41 BC to AD 68)
Period III	Roman military occupation (AD 68 until 73 or 74)

Jewish History after the Exile

Important Events in the Persian-Seleucid Period

All dates BC

539	Cyrus conquers Babylonia and permits Jews to return home
520	Jerusalem Temple rebuilt
334	Alexander begins invasion of Persian Empire
332	Alexander conquers Palestine
323	Alexander dies and his empire is divided
301	Ptolemaic rule over Palestine established
198	Seleucid rule over Palestine established
168	Antiochus IV forbids Jewish practices and builds an altar to Zeus in Jerusalem Temple
168–64	Maccabean Revolt
164	Re-dedication of the Temple under Judas Maccabeus

When seeking to understand ancient documents, whether the Dead Sea Scrolls or the New Testament, it is important to know a little about their historical setting.

The scrolls themselves shed very little light on their own historical setting. Hints within the scrolls to personalities and events are veiled by code names and poetic descriptions such as the 'Teacher of Righteousness'[6], the 'Wicked Priest'[7], 'the Liar'[8], 'those who look for smooth things'[9], and 'the builder of walls'[10].

The Historical Context

As we have seen, the experts agree that the scrolls were composed some time between 300 BC and AD 70, within the era often referred to as the 'intertestamental period', the time between the Old and New Testaments. However, this period is more accurately called the 'Second Temple' period, referring to the rebuilt Jewish Temple in Jerusalem. In 520 BC, shortly after their return from captivity in Babylon, the Jewish exiles rebuilt the Temple; it stood until the Romans destroyed it during the siege of Jerusalem in AD 70. Just before the fall of Jerusalem, the Qumran settlement was occupied by the Romans, although not before the scrolls were hidden in the caves.

As a background to the scrolls and Qumran, it is useful to outline the history of the Jewish people in Palestine from their captivity in Babylon to the time of the scrolls.

The Persians (539–334 BC)

In 586 BC, the Babylonians took the Jews into captivity (2 Chronicles 36:15–21; 2 Kings 25:1–21). In 518 BC, Cyrus, the Emperor of Persia, conquered the Babylonian Empire and allowed the Jews to return to Palestine and rebuild their Temple in Jerusalem (2 Chronicles 36:22–23). The Jews looked upon this so positively that they even referred to Cyrus as the Lord's 'Messiah' (Isaiah 45:1), and some viewed the return as a 'second Exodus'.

While for some Jews the return meant that God had fulfilled his promise to gather his people and reconstitute the nation of Israel, for others it was a false start. For the latter, the Temple was a shadow of its former glory and the people were signally failing to keep God's laws. They held out for a 'real' return and believed that a 'second Exodus' was still to come. The community of the scrolls aligned themselves with this view, believing that Israel, God's people, remained under the shadow of the exile, even if no longer literally in exile, since the nation was still under foreign domination and the people remained unrepentant.

The Seleucids (334–164 BC)

In 334 BC Alexander the Great defeated the Persians and, after his early death at the age of 32 in 323 BC, his empire was divided among four

An accurate model of the Second Temple showing how it dominated Jerusalem.

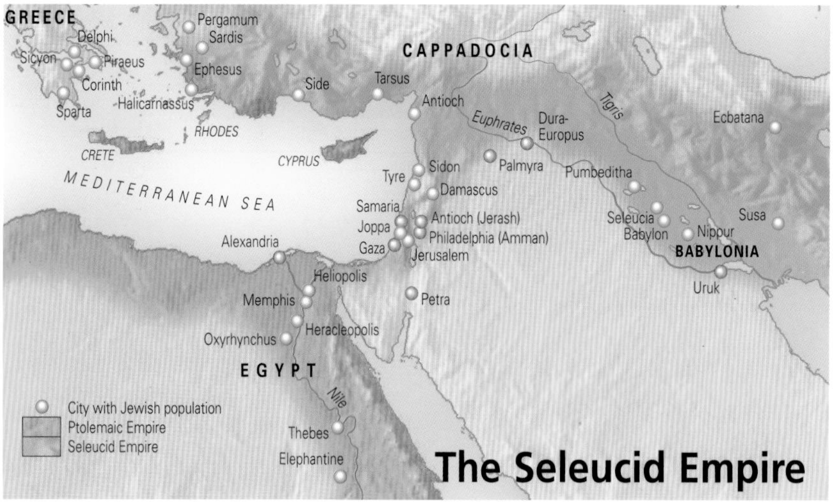
GREECE
Delphi
Sicyon
Piraeus
Corinth
Sparta
Pergamum
Sardis
Ephesus
Halicarnassus
RHODES
CRETE
Side
Tarsus
CAPPADOCIA
Antioch
Euphrates
Dura-Europus
Tigris
Ecbatana
CYPRUS
MEDITERRANEAN SEA
Tyre
Sidon
Palmyra
Pumbeditha
Damascus
Samaria
Joppa
Gaza
Antioch (Jerash)
Philadelphia (Amman)
Jerusalem
Seleucia
Babylon
Nippur
Susa
BABYLONIA
Uruk
Alexandria
Heliopolis
Memphis
Petra
Heracleopolis
Oxyrhynchus
EGYPT
Nile
Thebes
Elephantine
City with Jewish population
Ptolemaic Empire
Seleucid Empire

The Seleucid Empire

generals. Alexander's general Ptolemy ruled Egypt, and later added Palestine and Syria to his territories. Seleucus I, another of Alexander's four generals, ruled Babylonia, and in 198 BC, one of his successors, Antiochus III, defeated an Egyptian army and occupied Palestine.

The rule of the Seleucid king Antiochus IV brought dark days for Law-observant Jews in Palestine. Antiochus IV (also called Antiochus Epiphanes – 'Epiphanes' means 'God Manifest') attempted to spread Hellenism (Greek ideas and culture) in Palestine, converting Jerusalem into a Greek city, outlawing Jewish practices and Temple sacrifices, and desecrating the Temple by erecting an altar to Zeus (see a prophetic description of this in Daniel 9:27). The actions of Antiochus provoked a Law-observing Jew named Mattathias Maccabeus and his family to lead an armed revolt against the Seleucids, known as the Maccabean Revolt, which culminated in the establishment of a Jewish independent state – a 'golden age' for the Jewish people. The Maccabees were also known as the Hasmoneans, the designation of their dynasty.

The Hasmoneans (164–63 BC)

For a century, Jews living in Palestine were governed not by a foreign occupying power, but by their own Jewish monarchy. The Hasmoneans marked a high point for Jews who viewed this Jewish monarchy as the fulfilment of God's promises to restore the nation-state of Israel. This view was bolstered when the Hasmonean John Hyrcanus and his son Aristobulus I led major military campaigns and eventually secured the most extensive territory for the nation since Solomon's time. Subsequently, the Hasmoneans came to hold the offices of both high priest and king, which concerned some Jews, since the Hasmoneans were neither of a legitimate high-priestly family (i.e. the high-priestly family of Zadok) nor of Davidic royal descent.

During this period, Jewish sects established themselves and vied for political influence. The three (possibly among many) groups known to us through the New Testament and Josephus, the ancient Jewish historian, seem to have formed just before this period: the Sadducees, the Pharisees, and the Essenes (see box above). Most likely one of these sects was the collector, author, copier, and owner of the scrolls. The rise and fall of the Hasmoneans and the political and theological tensions that they created provide the historical context for the composition of the majority of the Dead Sea Scrolls.

Jewish Parties in the Second Temple Period

Sadducees A group comprising individuals with political and religious influence from the priesthood and upper classes. Their name is derived from the name 'Zadok', the high priest of the Jerusalem Temple in the time of Solomon. The Sadducees rejected the 'tradition of the fathers', or 'oral Torah', which Pharisees considered law on a par with the written Torah. Also, they were Roman sympathizers who wished to maintain the social and political status quo.

Pharisees As chief rival of the Sadducees, the Pharisees were the most influential and popular of the Jewish parties. They are said by Josephus to have numbered 6,000. Their name is derived from the Hebrew word *perushim*, which means 'separate'. They represented mainly the middle and lower classes and accepted the 'traditions of the fathers' – non-biblical laws, said to have been passed down orally through the generations. The Pharisees are thought to be the forebears of Rabbinic Judaism.

Essenes 4,000 dissenters from the Temple establishment because of its perceived impurity and corruption. They lived in small villages, where they resided communally, sharing possessions, meals and an ascetic lifestyle. Unlike the Pharisees and the Sadducees, the Essenes are not mentioned in the New Testament, although they had a centre in Jerusalem and would doubtless come in regular contact with the early Christian community.

Important Events in the Hasmonean Period

(All dates BC)

152	Jonathan becomes first Hasmonean ruler and assumes high priesthood
142	Jonathan murdered and succeeded by Simon
134–04	Simon murdered and succeeded by John Hyrcanus
104–03	Aristobulus I succeeds Hyrcanus
103–76	Alexander Janneus succeeds Aristobulus I
103	Qumran is inhabited by a splinter Essene group
76–67	Salome Alexander, widow of Alexander, succeeds her husband
67–63	Civil war between Salome's sons: Hyrcanus II and Aristobulus II
63	Roman conquest of Palestine by Pompey

Artist's impression of the new harbour city of Caesarea, built by Herod the Great and named in honour of his patron the Roman emperor.

The Romans (63 BC–AD 70)

The century of Jewish self-government was in reality far from a golden age. Internal rivalry between the Hasmoneans led to betrayal, brutality, and murder. Eventually things became so bad that the Roman general Pompey was invited by the Hasmoneans to settle their political disputes. In 63 BC Pompey assumed power over the Jews and entered Jerusalem, reportedly entering the Holy of Holies in the Temple, to the horror of devout Jews. Pompey installed a Roman governor but retained a Hasmonean as high priest.

Herod the Great

After several years of political unrest in the region, and an invasion from the east by the Parthians, Caesar Augustus appointed Herod (known as Herod the Great, see Matthew 2:1) as King of Israel in 37 BC Herod reigned for 34 years and became known as the greatest builder of his age. He constructed the new harbour city of Caesarea, named in honour of his patron the Roman emperor, and built many fortresses and residences for himself. Most notably, however, he undertook the renovation and enlargement of the Jerusalem Temple. Herod was Idumaean – a tribe in the southern part of Palestine forced by the Hasmoneans to adopt Judaism – and although he practiced a Jewish lifestyle, many Jews did not consider him a true Jew. Herod's renovation of the Temple may have been an attempt to win the favour of devout Jews.

Herod's Sons

After Herod's death, Rome eventually assumed direct control over the territory, which was initially divided among Herod's three sons, Philip, Herod Antipas, and Archelaus, although none was given the title of king. Archelaus was quickly deposed and Rome assumed direct administration over Judea, appointing rulers called prefects – such as Pontius Pilate – to keep the peace and collect taxes.

First Jewish Revolt

In the early part of the first century AD relations between the Romans and the Jews deteriorated greatly, until finally the Jews declared war on their Roman occupiers. The 'First Jewish Revolt' resulted in the Roman occupation of Jerusalem and the destruction of the Temple in AD 70. It was also during this time that the settlement at Qumran was attacked and occupied by the Romans, in AD 68.

The turbulent events that took place in the years between 300 BC and AD 70 form the backdrop to the writing of the Dead Sea Scrolls. Much of the sectarian literature is born out of the mainly negative interaction with the political, religious, social, and cultural régime created by the Hasmonean dynasty, the Roman occupation, and Herod the Great.

Jesus was born, lived, and died in the Palestine of the early first century. When he walked the land teaching, he spoke to political, economic, and social issues that were created by the Roman occupation and Herodian exploitation. Both the scrolls and the New Testament reflect the world of the first century.

The Community of the Scrolls

Scholars have made various suggestions concerning the identity of the community of the scrolls, most commonly naming the Sadducees, Pharisees, Temple priests, and the Essenes. The Essenes have proved to be the most convincing of these suggestions, and this remains the dominant view today, although it has undergone significant revision.

The Essenes are mentioned in classical Greek sources such as Pliny the Elder, Philo, and Josephus, whose description of them is strikingly similar to the group known from the scrolls. However, it is important to point out that no non-Greek sources mention the Essenes.

Similarities between the Essenes and the Qumran Community

1. Pliny referred to an Essene settlement on the western shore of the Dead Sea, a description that fits the location of the Qumran settlement.

2. Classical sources describe some of the beliefs of the Essenes, and these correspond to those mentioned in some of the scrolls. For example, Josephus says that a distinctive belief of the Essenes is that they 'leave everything in the hands of God' (*Ant.* 18:18). This deterministic theology is also reflected in the sectarian documents among the scrolls. For instance, the *Rule of the Community* (1QS) 3:15 states: 'All that is now and ever shall be originates with the God of knowledge'. Other beliefs mentioned by Josephus and also contained in the sectarian documents include the immortality

of the soul, the resurrection of the dead, and the future reward for the righteous.

3. The Greek sources depict peculiar practices that were characteristic of the Essenes and which are also reflected in the practices of the community described in the scrolls. Josephus notes many of these, perhaps because he thought his Roman readers would find them fascinating. Practices mentioned by Josephus and Philo and also described in the scrolls include:

a. prohibition of the use of oil [11]
b. prohibition against private property [12]
c. the eating of a common pure meal [13]
d. ceremonial bathing for ritual purity [14]
e. prohibition of spitting [15]
f. strict Sabbath observance [16]
g. specific oaths [17]
h. entry procedure when inducting new community members. [18]

This clay flask of balsam oil was discovered in a cave at Qumran.

There are, however, significant differences between the classical descriptions of the Essenes and the evidence from the scrolls. Most notably Josephus and Philo describe not a segregated-sectarian community, but one that was integrated into society and highly esteemed by the world. Yet the sectarian documents reveal a community at odds with the

Sun clock dial discovered at Qumran.

Remains of the Qumran settlement, with the cliffs beyond.

outside world and whose very existence is intended to act as a judgment on both the rest of Judaism and the Gentile world. It is difficult to imagine that such a group was highly esteemed.

Differences like this are very significant. Two other significant points need to be borne in mind:

1. Many of the scrolls were not composed by the community at Qumran.

2. Key documents among the scrolls are composite documents,

showing the presence of earlier sources that were incorporated and re-used in later sectarian documents.

Nevertheless, any hypothesis that seeks to understand the community behind the scrolls must take proper account of the sectarian nature of the documents found there. Some scholars claim that Qumran was something like a 'residential library' or a monastery for the wider Essene group, but this seems unlikely given the extreme views contained in some of the scrolls.

An Essene splinter-group?

The most convincing explanation of the identity of the group who resided at Qumran and collected, preserved, and in some cases wrote, the scrolls is that they were an Essene splinter-group. This view holds that the group at Qumran was an offshoot of the

parent Essene movement, and that ancient sources reveal at least two types of Essenes: Qumran Essenes and non-Qumran Essenes.

Grave of a Qumran Community member discovered at Ein Fashka, near the Dead Sea.

Whether the Qumran group would have continued to think of themselves as 'Essenes' is impossible to know, since this term is never used in any of the extant texts. The closest thing to a name for the community given in the scrolls is the Hebrew word *Yahad* meaning 'community' or 'union'.

The evidence from the Greek sources and the scrolls seems to suggest that the group was at one time related to the Essene movement, but later separated from it, and adhered to an extreme sectarian outlook. Possibly the Qumran group believed they were the truest form of the Essenes – the true Israel – and defined their identity in opposition to the parent movement. This view of the Qumran community as an Essene splinter-group is better able to explain the similarities and differences than any other hypothesis, although it remains only a hypothesis and as such is always subject to correction and revision.

The Essenes

The history of the Essenes probably begins in third-century BC Palestine, and is linked with the creation of apocalyptic literature, such as the Pseudepigraphic works of *Enoch* and *Jubilees* (see p. 12), which spoke of the end-times and God's final deliverance of Israel. This Jewish tradition became the foundation of the beliefs and practices of the Essenes, who we know existed prior to the reign of Jonathan Maccabeus

in 160–142 BC (Josephus *Ant*. 13.171). When the putative split in the movement took place is unclear – perhaps during the reign of the early Hasmoneans. However, archaeological evidence suggests that the group did not come to reside at Qumran until about 103 BC, in the reign of Alexander Janneus (see p. 20).

The Essenes split

The inter-Essene split was the result of a leader referred to in the scrolls

as the 'Teacher of Righteousness', whose identity is unknown, though he was possibly a high-ranking priest in the Jerusalem Temple. According to the scrolls, the Teacher of Righteousness was endowed with special inspiration for interpreting Scripture relating to the practice of the Jewish Law and events surrounding the end-times. A disagreement over his interpretation apparently ensued, and a small group of Essenes followed the Teacher and his interpretation, while the rest maintained the status quo and rejected the new leader. At some point during the life of the splinter sect the Teacher died, but the community continued to adhere to his teaching and to await the coming of the End of Days and the appearance of the Messiah.

Why this Essene splinter group chose to migrate to the Dead Sea is unknown, although it has been suggested that they felt called to act out a symbolical wilderness experience, like that of the Israelites under Moses, in preparation for the second Exodus, the deliverance of Israel and its restoration in the Promised Land.

Beliefs of the Qumran Community

The Dead Sea Scrolls are not simply a collection of one group's own writings. As we have noticed, some of the documents found in the caves around Qumran did not originate from the group that placed them there. In addition, even in the sectarian writings we can discern underlying layers which suggest that some of the key documents incorporate earlier traditions.

Yet, given the sectarian nature of the group who collected, preserved, and deposited the scrolls in the caves, it seems unlikely that they kept documents, or incorporated earlier sources, that expressed opinions different from their own. For this sectarian group, Jews whose beliefs and practices differed from theirs were not regarded as being merely in error or wrong, but as law-breakers outside God's covenant promise to Israel. All this suggests that documents that the community possessed would have been compatible with its own belief system.

On this assumption, it is possible to sketch the basic beliefs of the community under five topics: God, the End of Days, the Law, Israel, and the Messiah.

God

The Dead Sea Scroll community were above all devout Jews. Fundamental to their thinking was the person of Yahweh, who had revealed himself to Abraham, Isaac, Jacob, and Moses, and set apart Israel to be his own possession.

The central Scripture passage for Jews in this period, as today, was the *Shema*: Deuteronomy 6:4: '*Hear, O Israel: The Lord our God, the Lord is one*' (see p. 11). As early as the first century, devout Jews said the *Shema* along with the Ten Commandments as a prayer twice daily, in the morning and evening. This practice is alluded to in the scrolls in the *Rule of the Community* (1QS) 10:10: '*With the entry of the day and night I will enter the covenant of God, and at the exit of the evening and morning I will speak of His laws*'.

The *Shema* has been found on the parchment fragments from phylacteries (*tefillin*) and *mezuzot* found at Qumran (see p. 11). For Jews the *Shema* was and is a confession of the oneness and uniqueness their God: God is the Supreme Being, the creator and sustainer of all life. For the community, all reality began and ended with God. God is omnipotent and omniscient, and he predetermines events in history. The *Shema* formed the framework of the community's thinking and underpinned all that they believed. Thus, the Qumran Community was God-centred: all of life was seen with reference to God.

The End of Days

The phrase 'End of Days' is found often in the scrolls, and was used to express the Qumran Community's view of their historical situation. They believed that they were living in the last period of Israel's history before its final deliverance. With the appearance of the 'Teacher of

God

See, you are the prince of gods and the king of the glorious ones, lord of every spirit, ruler of every creature. Apart from you nothing happens, and nothing is known without your will. There is no one besides you, no one matches your strength, nothing equals your glory, there is no price on your might. And who among all your great creatures will have the strength to stand before your glory?
1QH^a 18:8–11

Remains of a potter's workshop at Qumran.

25

Righteousness' and the founding of their community, the 'End of Days' or 'last days' had arrived.

However, the Qumran Community viewed the 'End of Days' not as one climactic event of rescue, but as a two-stage process. The first stage would be the initial salvation of a small group, a remnant (called a 'plant root'[19]), who would undergo a time of testing and purification. The second stage was the appearance of the Messiah(s) and a final battle in which God's enemies would be judged and destroyed. In the community's view, since the first stage was currently being experienced, the coming of the Messiah(s) and the judgment of God were imminent.

The Law

The central issue for the Dead Sea Scrolls community was a person's

relationship to the Torah, the Law of Moses. The community understood the history of Israel to be a history of failure to maintain the covenant that God had made with them. At Sinai, God entered into a covenant relationship with Israel through the leadership of Moses that consisted of three parts:

1. Gracious deliverance from slavery and unconditional election.
2. Covenant stipulations.
3. Blessings and curses resulting from obedience or disobedience.

According to their retelling of Israel's history, the Qumran Community believed that the nation of Israel had failed to keep the covenant stipulations that they had committed to perform in response to God's election and gracious deliverance from Egypt. The result of this covenantal unfaithfulness was Israel's occupation, dispersion, and eventual exile from the Promised Land.

The community believed that this desperate situation was beginning to alter, and the long-awaited restoration of the nation had dawned in the founding of their community. What was required of Israel was repentance for their covenant unfaithfulness and a commitment to keep the revealed stipulations of Moses and follow the hidden law discerned in the message of the Teacher of Righteousness and the sons of Zadok.

For the Qumran Community there were two categories of Law: the revealed Law (Scripture) and the hidden Law (the sect's new interpretations). By joining the community, a person committed himself not only to keep the revealed Law found in the Torah and Prophets, but also the hidden Law that was being revealed to the leaders of the community through the inspired study of Scripture.

The hidden Law complemented

the revealed Law both by filling in gaps about important issues about which the Mosaic Law did not speak, and also by describing the events of the last days, which had been hidden from the biblical prophets. The community believed that it alone among the people of Israel correctly and faithfully followed the Torah and so was prepared for the imminent day of judgment and arrival of the Messiah.

Israel

The Qumran Community used the phrase 'people of God' in two ways: positively and negatively. Positively, the people of God were seen as those who will be delivered from end-time judgment and who in the present represented God's 'plant root' remnant in the Land. The people of God are also those who will be agents of God's judgment and the confidants of the Messiah. These are the true Israel.

Negatively, the people of God were described as evildoers, who would be judged along with the Gentile nations. The Messiah is pictured as coming against Jerusalem in judgment of those who have violated God's covenant with the Gentiles. There will be a 'day of slaughter', when the wicked among God's people will be wiped out. The scrolls imply that this is a large group in comparison with the remnant.

From the two senses in which 'the people of God' (or Israel) is used, we may conclude that the Qumran Community believed that there were two divergent futures for the people of God: one of judgment and one of salvation. Membership of the covenant community was essential to belong to the remnant, the true Israel. This membership grafted a person into God's new planting in the land, and the result was a firm hope of eschatological salvation.

The Qumran Community believed that, outside their

vation

for
ne,

Two Messiahs

The scrolls speak of two Messiahs who will appear together as the climax of 'the last days'. Their appearance will usher in the final restoration of Israel. One of the Messiahs is the long-awaited son of David. However, ancient Judaism could speak of numerous Messianic figures, since the word 'Messiah' simply translates the Hebrew term *mashiah*, 'anointed one'. Most Christians are only aware of the Davidic Messiah, but in ancient Jewish writings, end-time figures were called by the title Messiah without necessarily having a political or royal connotation. The 'Messiah of Aaron' is probably a reference to a priestly figure who will arise at the end of the present age.

The emphasis on a priestly Messiah, who according to the *War Scroll* is elevated over the royal Messiah in the end-time battle, could be seen as characteristic of

A close-up view of one of the Dead Sea Scrolls caves at Qumran.

the community's self-understanding as a priestly community. The community apparently believed that they were a temporary replacement of the corrupt Jerusalem Temple – a belief that helps explain their strict concern for purity and much of their community organization: they were

attempting to bring the purity of the Temple into their everyday lives.

Yet, the expectation of a dual Messiah, one priestly and one political, could have easily arisen from the Old Testament. The story of the simultaneous anointing of Solomon, the son of David, and of Zadok, the high priest, in 1 Chronicles 29:22, along with Zechariah's vision of the two 'sons of oil' (Zech. 4:14) could have led to such a belief in two Messiahs.

Life in the Qumran Community

The testimony of Eliezer ben Jonathan, an imaginary member[20].

My name is Eliezer ben Jonathan and I am 28 years old. I have been a member of the *Yahad* – that's what we call our community – for more than three years, and I want to tell you about my experience.

I grew up in a devout Jewish home in a village just outside our capital city, Jerusalem. My family have been members of the Essene sect for more than two generations, and the *Yahad* was formed about a century ago, when the Essene movement split. My grandfather, not being a radical, at first tried to remain neutral, but in the end sided with the majority Essene group.

An Essene childhood

From my early years, my parents taught me to read the Scripture and instilled into me the principles of the Essenes, and as a teenager I followed the Essene teachings they passed on to me. My father was a craftsman and I followed in his steps. We lived communally, sharing resources and helping our fellow members when anyone had need. We avoided luxury and riches because we saw them as a corrupting influence. Essenes have a very high reputation in the community; even Herod the Great respected some of our leaders. However, we were very concerned about ritual – outer – purity and for this reason looked on our fellow Jews with some suspicion, avoiding contact with certain people and things. We believed strongly that the centre of worship remained the Jerusalem Temple, but that the current priestly authority was not administering the sacrifices properly – so we continued to send our voluntary offerings to the Temple as prescribed, but did not participate in Temple worship.

As I entered my twenties I began to take my faith more seriously, becoming increasingly concerned about God's coming judgment and that the Essenes were unwilling to

Cutaway illustration of Qumran Settlement

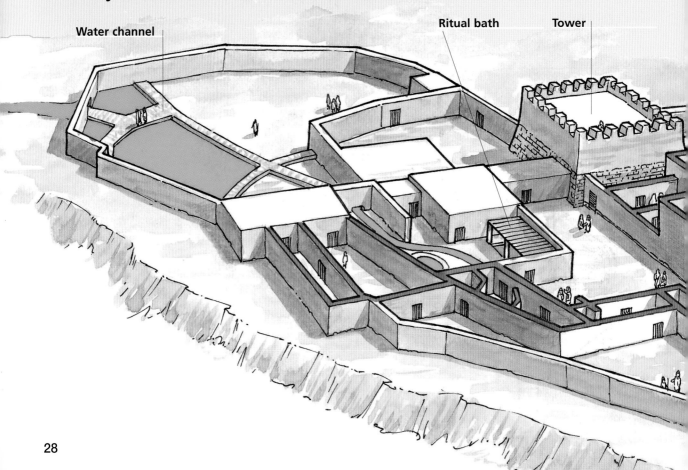

Water channel

Ritual bath

Tower

A New Covenant Community

In Jeremiah 31:31–34 God promises to make a new covenant with Israel in the future:

'The time is coming', declares the Lord, 'when I will make a new covenant with the house of Israel and with the house of Judah ... I will put my law in their hearts. I will be their God, and they will be my people ... For I will forgive their wickedness and will remember their sins no more.'

The Qumran Community believed that God had initiated the new covenant in the formation of their community. They were the new covenant community:

They should take care to act in accordance with the exact interpretation of the law for the age of wickedness ... according to what was discovered by *those who entered the new covenant* in the land of Damascus.
CD 6:19 [4Q266 frg. 3, II:1]

Righteousness', the founder of the *Yahad*. The most powerful thing he said to me – the thing God most used to change my life – was:

Israel is unfaithful to God; they have been so from the very beginning of their history, and remain so today. Yes – the Temple was rebuilt, but God's presence is not there. The priesthood is corrupt and God is displeased. The only chance you have to escape God's judgment when he returns to restore Israel's kingdom is to join our community; there is no redemption outside our *Yahad*! No longer is it enough to be an Israelite, you must repent of your sins and join the new covenant God has made with our *Yahad*.

I had never met a man so serious and single-minded. And, though I was taken aback by his exclusive claims, what he said had the ring of truth.

challenge the religious leaders in Jerusalem for their wrong administration of the Temple. It seemed that, while the Essenes believed that God would soon come to redeem Israel and judge the unfaithful among our people, they were not willing to separate completely from the impure and their practices.

I became intrigued by the *Yahad*, which now resided in the Judean wilderness on the Dead Sea. I happened to meet one of its members – not a common occurrence – and discussed his beliefs. I learned that they were an all-male society who observed the Law very strictly. They believed they should not only obey the Torah, but also the teachings of 'the Teacher of

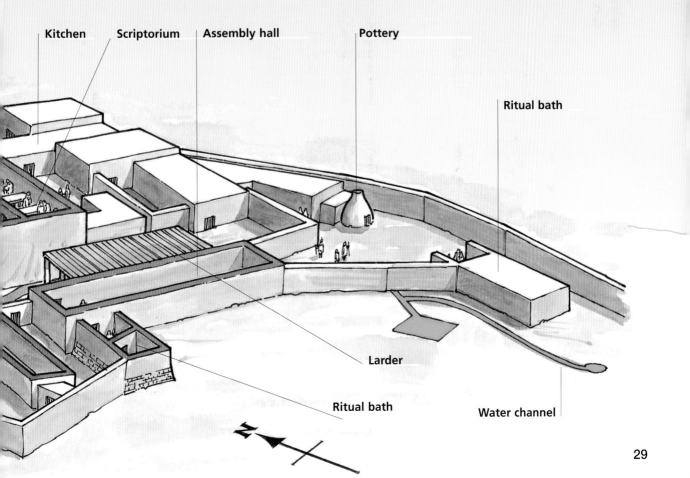

Kitchen   Scriptorium   Assembly hall   Pottery

Ritual bath

Larder

Ritual bath

Water channel

I join the Yahad

Finally, after much prayer – and many tears – I left my family and village to join the *Yahad*. It was the hardest decision of my life. But I believe God is sovereign and I knew I was meant to join the *Yahad*. My overwhelming desire was – and is – to please God and be prepared for his future redemption. I was sad to leave my family – of course, they didn't understand – but more than anything else I want to experience the new kingdom that God will bring when he rescues Israel. I just hope one day my family will join me in the *Yahad*.

However, you can't just join the *Yahad*. I had to undergo a two-year initiation before I received full membership. First I was brought before the leader, who asked a series of questions about my observance of the Torah (the Law of Moses) and my conduct. He was trying to gauge my understanding of Torah and my faithfulness to it. Although I was very nervous, I felt that I understood the Torah and knew I had struggled to live out God's laws. I knew I wasn't perfect, but God does not demand sinless perfection – only that I repent of my transgression when I sin. I believe God graciously and unconditionally chose Israel to be his people and delivered them from bondage in Egypt. In that act, we became his people and he our God. In this relationship, God forgives those that truly repent of their sins. So, whenever I sin, I humbly seek his forgiveness and repent of my transgression of his law. This is life under God's Torah.

My induction

After that initial interview, which thankfully I passed, I was allowed to receive instruction from the teachers and priests. This was the first stage of my induction into the community.

I received regular instruction on the 'hidden' things in the Scripture that had been revealed to the Teacher of Righteousness in these last days. The Teacher was God's special messenger whom he raised up to prepare his true people for the last days and the appearance of the Messiah. During these first few months, I had very little contact with members of the *Yahad*. I was not allowed to eat with them, and certainly not to drink with them, as we believe impurity is most easily passed through liquids. Only the purest can drink together. I know it might sound a bit weird – but this is what we believe.

After several months, I was brought before the whole community and my progress was evaluated. *Yahad* members determined my suitability for membership, based on my understanding and application of the teaching I had received. This was very intimidating, as I was questioned before the whole community of about 100 people. Providentially, the *Yahad* deemed I

had progressed sufficiently to be given provisional membership of the community, though I still had limited privileges. For example, I was still barred from the common 'pure meal' with members and I had no right to the use the common property of the community.

In these early days, I often felt very lonely and inadequate. The process of initiation is designed to move a person through higher levels of purity until they are 'ritually pure'; only at this highest stage of purity are they ready for membership. I wondered if I would ever achieve the level of purity required for full membership. Ritual purification was not simply an outward reality, as some outsiders think; we believe that ritual purity and impurity are an outward sign of the inward reality of a person. In other words, who you are outside says a lot about who you are inside.

After the first year – it felt like an eternity – I appeared again for assessment before the leadership of the *Yahad*. Again, I was asked a

The Community's Punishments

There were strict punishments for members breaking the community's code of conduct. Here are some of the offences and their punishments:

Offence	Punishment
Misuse of divine name	Permanent expulsion
Informing against the sect	Expulsion
Complaining against sect	Separation from the teachings of the pure food for one year. Reduction of food ration by a quarter for two years. Separation from pure drink for two years
Speaking angrily against priests Intentionally insulting another Knowingly lying about money Gossiping against one's fellow	Separation from pure food and reduction of food ration by a quarter for one year
Falling asleep during the community's meetings Missing a vote Spitting in the meeting Laughing loudly and foolishly	Reduction of food ration by a quarter for 30 days

Chart adapted from Schiffman 1994: 109.

Aerial view of the remains of the settlement at Qumran.

battery of questions and my behaviour was scrutinized. The leaders were assessing whether I was suitable for the next, and final, stage of the initiation process. After a long and gruelling examination, I was sent from the room to await their decision. Then I was invited back, and informed by the leader that I had made good progress and was worthy of a higher level of membership.

I will never forget that day. I had not completed my initiation, but had come a long way. I was now able to eat the 'pure meal' with the rest of the members, and I turned over my possessions to the examiner who would look after them. Once I had completed the second year of initiation, my possessions would be shared among the *Yahad*. Then, not only would I be able to share in the common possessions of the community, but also I would finally be allowed to drink with them.

Full membership at last!

Finally, after two years I was inducted into the *Yahad* with full membership privileges. My name was recorded in the register of the new covenant community and I was given a rank within the community that reflected my knowledge of Torah, the foundational principles of the community, and my knowledge of ritual purity. It was a great day!

Since becoming a full member a year ago, I have continued to grow in my understanding of God and find great joy in preparing for the arrival of Messiah.

I have come to learn that the purpose of all the *Yahad*'s rules and principles is to live in the present in a way that reflects the coming future. We believe that in these last days that God's future kingdom has broken into the present, and as a community we reflect that future reality by living pure lives.

I really love life in the *Yahad*. I live outside the settlement, like most of my brothers, in a cave with a fellow member. My days are filled with prayers, common meals, study, regular purification baths, *Yahad* business meetings or assemblies, and, of course, work – I help make the pottery which is produced right here in our settlement.

While you may regard the *Yahad* as 'legalistic' or 'fundamentalist', I believe with all my heart that God is coming soon finally to redeem his true people, Israel. At that time he will judge not only the pagan idolaters who do not know God, but also any of the people of Israel who are not spiritually prepared for his arrival. God has raised up the Teacher of Righteousness and the *Yahad* in these last days to be his means to restore the nation of Israel. I want to participate in that redemption.

The New Testament and the Scrolls

Bizarre claims

In the years since the discovery of the scrolls, many outlandish claims have been made for the connection between Christianity and the scrolls. For example, a few scholars have argued that Jesus was a sort of 'secret agent' for the Essenes, or that New Testament documents were found among the scrolls.[21] More radically, one scholar has argued that figures mentioned in the scrolls refer cryptically to New Testament figures: John the Baptist was the 'Teacher of Righteousness' and Jesus the 'Wicked Priest'. Yet another writer suggested that the New Testament is a book of codes that needs to be deciphered by a technique similar to *pesher* exegesis (see p. 15 on the definition of pesher). Some writers have tried to link the Dead Sea Scrolls and the New Testament with New Age philosophy and ideas about reincarnation. John Allegro, a member of the original scrolls editorial team, even asserted that the scrolls provide evidence of the existence of a mystical tradition connected with a hallucinogenic mushroom, from which the myth of Jesus arose.

The scrolls and the New Testament

In spite of these bizarre suggestions, most scholars today agree that there is no direct relationship between the Dead Sea Scrolls and the New Testament. However, there is certainly literary, archaeological, and historical evidence that makes it likely that the Essenes, the Qumran Community's parent movement, and early Christians did interact. It is likely that Jesus was as familiar with the Essenes as he was with the Sadducees and Pharisees, although strangely the Gospels never mention them. While we should not read too much from silence, this absence does raise the possibility of a close connection between the early Christians and the Essenes. In addition, there is archaeological evidence to suggest there was an Essene centre in Jerusalem close to the early Christian community.[22] Descriptions of early Christian converts in the book of Acts may reflect Essene identity (see Acts 6:7).

So, although no evidence can be found that directly links the Qumran Community with early Christianity, there is good reason to suppose there was considerable interaction between the Essenes and Christians. If this is the case, we can hypothecate at least an indirect relationship between scrolls and the New Testament. The extent of that relationship however is impossible to determine.

John the Baptist and Qumran

Further, given that both John the Baptist and Jesus spent a significant amount of time in the Judean Wilderness, it is reasonable to assume that they had knowledge, if not first-hand experience, of the Qumran Community. It even seems possible that John the Baptist may have had some relationship with Qumran. There are interesting links between John and the Dead Sea Scrolls community. For example, John's family background, the location of his ministry, his interpretation of Scripture, and his urgent kingdom message all find parallels in the scrolls. However, these parallels fall short of confirming a direct link between John the Baptist and Qumran.

Qumran and the early church

There are important similarities between the beliefs of the Qumran Community as expressed in the scrolls and those of the early church seen from the New Testament. For instance, both groups were early first century Palestinian Jewish Messianic movements. Both groups

Archaeologist Shimon Gibson points to ancient wall carvings in a cave where he believes John the Baptist anointed many of his followers.

Scale model of the inner courts and main sanctuary of Herod's Temple.

of their community and that at the appearance of Messiah the covenant will be brought to its full realization.

5. Both groups share a similar view of the **Jerusalem Temple**, seeing their own community as a human Temple replacing the present earthly Temple, at least for a time.

6. Both groups handle some **biblical texts** similarly, which suggests a **tradition of interpretation** shared by both groups – examples of such shared interpretation include: Isaiah 61:1–2 in Luke 7:22 and 4Q521 (*Messianic Apocalypse*), and the Parable of the Vineyard in Matthew 21:33–42, Mark 12:1–12 and 4Q500.

The Teacher of Righteousness

The role of the Teacher of Righteousness for the Qumran Community in the scrolls is similar to Jesus' role for the early church in the New Testament. According to the belief of each group, God raised up a person and endowed him with new revelation for the last days. This new revelation did not replace the former revelation of Israel's scripture, but complemented and intensified it in view of the End of Days. The new revelation, and intensified interpretation of old revelation in the light of his coming is what distinguished the early church, the sect of the Nazarenes, from others in ancient Judaism.

In addition, the scrolls and the New Testament reveal a shared language that points to a common conceptual world. Examples of this shared language are some of the words and phrases that appear in both sets of documents: children of light, the righteousness of God, works of the Law, lawlessness, light and darkness, Belial, and the human Temple of God.

shared the dynamic expectation of a soon-coming Messiah. Most people assume that every Jew at the time of Jesus was looking for a Messiah; however, while Messianism was growing in the early first century, the historical evidence does not support this assumption. It is true that the specific beliefs of the Qumran Community and the early church about the Messiah differed – for example, the scrolls speak of two Messiahs – but the shared expectation of a Messiah is an important similarity that should not be quickly passed over.

In their similar identities as Jewish Messianic movements, the documents reveal other striking theological similarities between Qumran and the early church:

1. Both share a **dualistic cosmology** – a view of the world and reality that is divided between good and evil, darkness and light.

2. Both share a similar understanding of the '**End of Days**' as a two-stage process first of testing and then triumph.

3. Both groups insist that they are the **true Israel** and that outside their individual community no salvation is available for Israel.

4. Both groups believe that the **new covenant** of Jeremiah 31:31–34 has been inaugurated in the formation

Early Christianity and Qumran

All this evidence reveals a relationship between the scrolls and the New Testament, and between early Christianity and the Qumran Community. However, no more than an indirect relationship can be affirmed. There are at least three reasons a direct relationship between them is not plausible:

1. Many of the similarities suggested above can be explained by the fact that both groups derive from a first-century Palestinian Jewish setting and both rooted their identity in the Torah, Prophets, and Writings – Israel's Scripture. Given their shared environment and fundamental theological resource, it is not surprising that early Christianity shared practices and perspectives with other Jewish groups in the first century.

2. No archaeological or literary evidence exists that clearly connects the two groups. Some scholars have made claims to the contrary, but their arguments are often based more on subjective reconstructions than on hard historical evidence. *No evidence of the New Testament or of Jesus currently exists in the scrolls.*

3. The early Christian view of Jesus and his Messianic identity sets Christians apart from all other Jewish groups and especially from the Qumran Community. For the early Christians, Jesus of Nazareth was Israel's Messiah and as such he was not merely the human agent of God's end-time redemption. Rather Jesus was proclaimed by Christians to be God himself: Jesus, the Messiah, was coequal with God the Father (John 10:30).

In addition, Jesus, the Messiah, was crucified on a Roman cross and Christians claimed his death was an atoning sacrifice for Israel's sins. Jesus was not in the first instance the triumphal king of the prophets

Some of the Dead Sea Scrolls on display in the Shrine of the Book, Jerusalem. The display cabinet is modelled on the handle of a scroll, and the museum building on the distinctive lid of the scroll jars.

(see Isaiah 9, 11) who would reign over Israel's kingdom forever on the throne of his father David. Instead, he was the suffering servant of Isaiah 53 who atoned for the sins of Israel through his death.

The New Testament, and indeed Jesus himself, conceived of the end-time Messiah in terms of *both* a suffering servant and a triumphal king. This Messianic vision was apparently novel among Jews in the first century, but by no means alien to the expectations revealed in the Old Testament. What distinguished Jesus and his early Jewish believers from all other Jews in the middle decades of the first century was their interpretation and application of the Jewish Scriptures to both Jesus' Messianic mission and their end-time community identity.

Notes

1 *The Meaning of the Dead Sea Scrolls* (VanderKam and Flint 2002: 22),
2 Brian Webster in Tov 2002: 371–75
3 Attached to the *Community Rule* found in Cave 1 were two additional small documents that are normally considered separate compositions: *The Rule of the Congregation* and *Blessings* (1QSa, 1QSb)
4 *The Archaeology of Qumran and the Dead Sea Scrolls*
5 2002: 105–62
6 CD 1:10–11; 1QpHab 7:1–5
7 1QpHab 8:3–13
8 1QpHab 20:10–15
9 CD 1:14–21; 4Q177; 4Q163
10 CD 5:6–9
11 Jos. *War* 2.123/4QMMT
12 *War* 2.8.2; 122; Philo's *Every Man is Free*, 85-87/ 1QS 6:18-23
13 *War* 2:8:5; 129–31/1QS 5:13–14
14 *War* 2:158; *Ant.* 18:18-20/1QS 3:7–10
15 *War* 2.8.9; 147/1QS 7:13
16 *War* 2.8.9; 147/CD 10–11
17 *War* 2.139/1QS 5:7–8
18 *War* 2.137–42/ 1QS 6:16–18
19 CD 1:4–11
20 Information used to create this imaginary portrait of sectarian life was drawn from the foundation documents of the scrolls, such as the *Rule of the Community*, the *Damascus Document* and the *Halakhic Letter*
21 Most recently Dan Brown in *The Da Vinci Code*
22 Riesner 1992

The Scrolls and the Christian

While it is true that there has been no amazing discovery of New Testament documents or specific information about Jesus and his Jewish believers among the scrolls, this does not diminish the importance of the scrolls for Christians. The more we read the scrolls, absorb their language and concepts and perceive their historical setting and worldview, the better we will appreciate how Jesus and the New Testament were inextricably linked with the faith of the Jews.

Our Jewish heritage

We will also learn that our Christianity is not a religion distinct from the ancient Jewish faith. Our hope as twenty-first century Christians is still the same as it was for those first Jewish believers: the final redemption of God's people, Israel. Only through the salvation of Israel will salvation come to the Gentiles, the non-Jewish world.

The forgiveness of sins and our future salvation that comes through a personal relationship with Jesus is nothing less than the fulfilment of God's ancient promise to Abraham in Genesis 12:3b: 'and all the peoples of the earth will be blessed through you'.

Christian distinctives

On the other hand, a study of the scrolls also teaches us where the Christian faith departs from other Jewish expressions. The Christian faith is a distinct form of Jewish faith because it believes that, in Jesus of Nazareth, God kept his ancient promises to redeem Israel, which he accomplished personally and actively by becoming a Jewish person and entering into the history of his people. According to the early Jewish believers – and as affirmed by all true Christians through history – Jesus is 'Immanuel, God with us' (Matthew 1:23).

Copyright © 2008 Lion Hudson plc/ Tim Dowley Associates

Published in 2010 by Kregel Publications, a division of Kregel, Inc., P.O. Box 2607, Grand Rapids, Michigan, 49501.

All rights reserved. No part of this publication may be reproduced, stored in a retrieval system, or transmitted in any form—for example, electronic, photocopy, recording—without the written prior permission of the publisher. The only exceptions are brief quotations in printed reviews.

Worldwide co-edition produced by:
Lion Hudson plc
Wilkinson House,
Jordan Hill Road
Oxford OX2 8DR England
Tel: +44 (0) 1865 302750

Fax: +44 (0) 1865 302757
Email: coed@lionhudson.com
www.lionhudson.com

ISBN: 978-0-8254-4196-7

Printed in China

Picture acknowledgments:
Photographs
Israel Government Press Office: front cover, pp. 2, 4, 6, 7, 8, 9, 11 right, 12, 13, 16 bottom, 22, 24, 27, 32, 34
Three's Company: pp. 5, 11 left, 14, 16 top, 18, 19, 23, 25, 33, back cover
Zev Radovan: p. 31

Illustrations
Brian Bartles: p. 21
Peter Dennis: pp. 4, 10, 15
Jeremy Gower: pp. 28–29
Richard Scott: p. 3

Index

Resources for Studying the Dead Sea Scrolls

English Translations

García Martínez, Florentino. *The Dead Sea Scrolls Translated: The Qumran Texts in English*. 1996. Leiden; Grand Rapids: Brill; Eerdmans.

Parry, Donald W. and Emanuel Tov, eds. *The Dead Sea Scrolls Reader*. 2004–2005. Leiden: Brill.

Vermès, Géza. *The Complete Dead Sea Scrolls in English*. 1998. London: Penguin Books.

General Introductions to the Scrolls and Reference Works

Davies, Philip R., George J. Brooke, and Phillip R. Callaway. *The Complete World of the Dead Sea Scrolls*. 2002. London: Thames & Hudson. This is a very good introduction to the scrolls and the most pictorial.

Helyer, Larry R. *Exploring Jewish Literature of the Second Temple Period: A Guide for New Testament Students*, pp. 180–275. 2002. Downers Grove: InterVarsity Press. The two chapters on the scrolls are a very useful introduction to the subject from an Evangelical perspective.

Knibb, Michael A. *The Qumran Community*. CCWJCW 2. 1987. Cambridge: Cambridge University Press. This is an older work, but a very good commentary on many of the key documents in the scrolls.

Schiffman, Lawrence H. *Reclaiming the Dead Sea Scrolls: The History of Judaism, the Background of Christianity, the Lost Library of Qumran*. 1994. Philadelphia: Jewish Publication Society. This good introduction to the scrolls is written by a prominent Jewish scholar who wishes to explain their significance for understanding Judaism.

Schiffman, Lawrence H. and James C. VanderKam, eds. *Encyclopedia of the Dead Sea Scrolls*. 2000. New York: Oxford University Press. This reference work contains a wealth of information on just about any topic related to the scrolls and Qumran.

Tov, Emanuel, ed. *The Texts from the Judean Desert: Indices and Introduction to the Discoveries in the Judean Desert Series*. DJD. 2002. Oxford: Clarendon Press.

VanderKam, James and Peter Flint. *The Meaning of the Dead Sea Scrolls: Their Significance for Understanding the Bible, Judaism, Jesus, and Christianity*. 2002. New York: HarperCollins. This book is a very useful and accessible introduction to the scrolls. It provides a detailed and up-to-date discussion of the scrolls with special emphasis on the history of the formation of the biblical text.

'Qumran and the Dead Sea Scrolls: Discoveries, Debates, The Scrolls and the Bible', 2000. *Near Eastern Archaeological Society Bulletin* 63, no. 3. This periodical is an excellent introduction to the scrolls with lots of pictures and diagrams.

Archaeology of Qumran

Magness, Jodi. *The Archaeology of Qumran and the Dead Sea Scrolls*. 2002. Studies in the Dead Sea Scrolls and Related Literature. Grand Rapids: Eerdmans. The best introduction to the archaeology of Qumran.

Hirschfeld, Yizhar. *Qumran in Context: Reassessing the Archaeological Evidence*. 2004. Peabody, MA: Hendrickson. This work is by a well-respected Israeli archaeologist who seeks to critique the widely held sectarian settlement interpretation of Qumran.

Essenes

Beall, Todd S. *Josephus' Description of the Essenes Illustrated by the Dead Sea Scrolls*. 1988. Cambridge: Cambridge University Press.

Riesner, Rainer. 'Jesus, the Primitive Community, and the Essene Quarter of Jerusalem', in *Jesus and the Dead Sea Scrolls*, ed. James H. Charlesworth, pp. 198–234. 1992. ABRL. New York: Doubleday. This essay argues that there was a close relationship between the Essenes and early Christians in Jerusalem.

Vermès, Géza, and Martin D. Goodman. *The Essenes According to Classical Sources*. 1989. Sheffield: Sheffield Academic Press. A short resource providing all the ancient citations about the Essenes.

The New Testament and the Scrolls

Brooke, George J. *Qumran and the Jewish Jesus*. Grove Biblical Series. 2005. Cambridge: Grove Books. A short and accessible introduction to the relationship between the New Testament and the scrolls by a well-known scrolls scholar.

Charlesworth, James H., ed. *Jesus and the Dead Sea Scrolls*. 1992. ABRL. New York: Doubleday. An important series of essays by eminent scholars on the relationship between the New Testament and the scrolls.

Collins, John J. *The Scepter and the Star: The Messiahs of the Dead Sea Scrolls and Other Ancient Literature*. 1995. ABRL. New York: Doubleday. The best book available on Messianism in the Dead Sea Scrolls.

Thiede, Carsten Peter. *The Dead Sea Scrolls and the Jewish Origins of Christianity*. 2000. Oxford: Lion Publishing. A useful resource for students interested in the relationship between the New Testament and Qumran.

Web Sites for Scrolls Study

Searching Google for 'Dead Sea Scrolls' brings up about 797,000 hits. Here are a handful of sites I found helpful:

Scrolls from the Dead Sea, an Exhibit at the Library of Congress, Washington D.C.
http://www.ibiblio.org/expo/deadsea.scrolls.exhibit/intro.html

Orion Canter for the Study of the Dead Sea Scrolls
http://orion.mscc.huji.ac.il/

What is the importance of the Dead Sea Scrolls?
http://www.christiananswers.net/q-abr/abr-a023.html

The Essenes and the Dead Sea Scrolls at Qumran
http://members.aol.com/Wisdomway/deadseascrolls.htm

General Dead Sea Scrolls Information
http://home.flash.net/~hoselton/deadsea/deadsea.htm#top
http://encyclopedia.com/html/d/deads1eas1.asp
http://www.abu.nb.ca/Courses/NTIntro/InTest/Qumran.htm
http://www.brandx.net/dbajot/deadsea/
http://www.otgateway.com/deadseascrolls.htm
http://www.abc.net.au/religion/features/scrolls/about.htm
http://mosaic.lk.net/g-qumran.html

The Israel Museum
http://www.imj.org.il/eng/shrine/introduction.html

300 Dead Sea Scroll Sites
http://www.mysteries-megasite.com/main/bigsearch/dead-sea.html

James Tabor's Website
http://www.religiousstudies.uncc.edu/jdtabor/dss.html